CAT BREEDS

BRITISH SHORTHAIRS

BY ABBY DOTY

WWW.APEXEDITIONS.COM

Copyright © 2025 by Apex Editions, Mendota Heights, MN 55120. All rights reserved. No part of this book may be reproduced or utilized in any form or by any means without written permission from the publisher.

Apex is distributed by North Star Editions:
sales@northstareditions.com | 888-417-0195

Produced for Apex by Red Line Editorial.

Photographs ©: Shutterstock Images, cover, 1, 4–5, 6, 8–9, 10–11, 12, 14–15, 18, 19, 20–21, 22–23, 24, 25, 26–27, 29; iStockphoto, 16–17

Library of Congress Control Number: 2024940532

ISBN
979-8-89250-308-2 (hardcover)
979-8-89250-346-4 (paperback)
979-8-89250-421-8 (ebook pdf)
979-8-89250-384-6 (hosted ebook)

Printed in the United States of America
Mankato, MN
012025

NOTE TO PARENTS AND EDUCATORS

Apex books are designed to build literacy skills in striving readers. Exciting, high-interest content attracts and holds readers' attention. The text is carefully leveled to allow students to achieve success quickly. Additional features, such as bolded glossary words for difficult terms, help build comprehension.

TABLE OF CONTENTS

CHAPTER 1
PLAYING AND PURRING 4

CHAPTER 2
HUNTING CATS 10

CHAPTER 3
CALM CATS 16

CHAPTER 4
CAT CARE 22

COMPREHENSION QUESTIONS • 28
GLOSSARY • 30
TO LEARN MORE • 31
ABOUT THE AUTHOR • 31
INDEX • 32

CHAPTER 1

PLAYING AND PURRING

A British shorthair plays with a ball. He bats it around the room. Then, he hears a door open. His owner is home. The cat runs to her.

British shorthairs are good at entertaining themselves. They may run around or play with toys.

The owner picks up a feather wand toy. She waves it back and forth. The cat jumps up and grabs it.

FAST FACT
British shorthairs tend to play in short bursts a few times a day.

◀ **British shorthairs used to be hunting cats. Today, many enjoy chasing and catching toys.**

After playing, the owner sits on the couch. The cat curls up nearby. He begins to **purr**. Soon, the owner and cat fall asleep.

LOUD PURRS

British shorthairs don't meow often. However, the cats may purr when happy. And some purr loudly. In fact, British shorthairs have set records for their loud purrs.

British shorthairs may sleep up to 20 hours in a day.

CHAPTER 2

Hunting Cats

The **Roman Empire** spread to Britain nearly 2,000 years ago. Romans brought cats to hunt **rodents**. These street cats stayed in Britain after the Romans left.

Roman ruins can still be found throughout Britain.

For hundreds of years, the street cats mixed with other wild cats. Their fur became thicker. They **developed** round and **stocky** bodies. By the 1800s, people kept the cats as pets.

FAST FACT
British shorthairs were part of the world's first cat show in 1871.

◀ Thick coats helped British shorthairs stay warm and dry outside.

During World War II (1939–1945), British shorthairs almost died out. But people worked to save them. Today, British shorthairs are **popular** around the world.

BOUNCING BACK

After World War II, few British shorthairs remained. People mixed these cats with other **breeds** that had similar looks. This helped British shorthairs bounce back. By the 1970s, they were popular again.

Russian blues have short, gray fur. After World War II, people mixed them with British shorthairs.

CHAPTER 3

CALM CATS

British shorthairs are fairly large cats. Some weigh up to 17 pounds (8 kg). They have strong bodies and wide chests.

British shorthairs have round heads and cheeks.

Many British shorthairs have orange eyes.

All British shorthairs have short, thick fur. Many have blue-gray coats. But the cats come in several other colors and patterns.

FAST FACT
British shorthairs were once called British blues.

British shorthairs' coat colors include shades of orange, white, and brown.

British shorthairs are calm and easygoing. The cats do well in many types of homes. They get along with other pets. And most are good with children.

SHY AND SWEET

British shorthairs may be timid around new people. The cats can take time to get comfortable. Then, they become very **loyal** and loving. They are sweet and friendly cats.

British shorthairs can do well in small apartments.

CHAPTER 4

CAT CARE

Owners should brush their British shorthairs once a week. The cats shed more during spring and fall. They may need more brushing then.

British shorthairs' fur gets longer and thicker in winter. That helps the cats stay warm.

British shorthairs can get exercise by climbing on cat furniture.

British shorthairs are fairly active and playful cats. But they also enjoy lying around. The cats can gain weight easily. So, owners should make sure their cats exercise every day.

FAST FACT
Owners should feed most cats two small meals each day.

Measuring out meals prevents British shorthairs from overeating.

Owners should try to play with their British shorthairs a few times a day.

British shorthairs are adaptable cats. They like being with people. But they can stay by themselves for several hours. They make good pets for busy people or families.

NOT FOR LAPS

British shorthairs enjoy attention. But most are not lap cats. They may not like to be picked up, hugged, or cuddled too much.

COMPREHENSION QUESTIONS

Write your answers on a separate piece of paper.

1. Write a few sentences explaining the main ideas of Chapter 3.

2. Would you like to own a British shorthair? Why or why not?

3. When was the world's first cat show?
    - A. 1871
    - B. 1945
    - C. 2011

4. Why would British shorthairs make good cats for busy people?
    - A. The cats can live totally outdoors.
    - B. The cats need to be with people at all times.
    - C. The cats can be alone for a few hours.

5. What does **timid** mean in this book?

*British shorthairs may be **timid** around new people. The cats can take time to get comfortable.*

    A. fearful and shy
    B. friendly right away
    C. not able to learn

6. What does **adaptable** mean in this book?

*British shorthairs are **adaptable** cats. They like being with people. But they can stay by themselves for several hours.*

    A. not comfortable around people
    B. comfortable in only one setting
    C. okay in several different settings

Answer key on page 32.

GLOSSARY

breeds
Specific types of cats that have their own looks and abilities.

developed
Changed over time.

loyal
Loving and staying true to a person or thing.

popular
Liked by or known to many people.

purr
To make a low, vibrating sound.

rodents
Small, furry animals with large front teeth, such as rats or mice.

Roman Empire
A huge empire that ruled parts of Europe, Asia, and Africa. It lasted from 27 BCE to 476 CE.

stocky
Wide and sturdy.

TO LEARN MORE

BOOKS

Jaycox, Jaclyn. *Read All About Cats*. North Mankato, MN: Capstone Publishing, 2021.

Klukow, Mary Ellen. *British Shorthair Cats*. Mankato, MN: Amicus, 2020.

Pearson, Marie. *Cat Behavior*. Minneapolis: Abdo Publishing, 2024.

ONLINE RESOURCES

Visit **www.apexeditions.com** to find links and resources related to this title.

ABOUT THE AUTHOR

Abby Doty is a writer, editor, and booklover from Minnesota.

A
active, 24

B
ball, 4
bodies, 13, 16
breeds, 14
Britain, 10
brush, 22

E
exercising, 24

F
feather wand toy, 7
fur, 13, 18

L
loyal, 20

M
meals, 25

O
owners, 4, 7–8, 22, 24–25

P
playing, 4, 7–8, 24
purring, 8–9

R
rodents, 10
Roman Empire, 10

S
shedding, 22

W
World War II, 14

ANSWER KEY:
1. Answers will vary; 2. Answers will vary; 3. A; 4. C; 5. A; 6. C